W9-ANY-026

CONTAINER TOPIARY

CONTAINER TOPIARY

SUSAN BERRY

Photographs by Steven Wooster

NEW HOLLAND

This edition first published in 2008 by
New Holland Publishers (UK) Ltd
London • Cape Town • Sydney • Auckland

Garfield House
86–88 Edgware Road
London W2 2EA
United Kingdom
www.newhollandpublishers.com

80 McKenzie Street
Cape Town 8001
South Africa

Unit 1, 66 Gibbes Street
Chatswood
NSW 2067
Australia

218 Lake Road
Northcote
Auckland
New Zealand

10 9 8 7 6 5 4 3 2 1

Copyright © 2003 New Holland Publishers (UK) Ltd
Text copyright © 2003 Susan Berry
Illustrations copyright © 2003 New Holland Publishers (UK) Ltd
Photography copyright © 2003 Susan Berry

Susan Berry has asserted her moral right to be identified as the author of this work. All rights
reserved. No part of this publication may be reproduced, stored in a retrieval system, or transmitted
in any form or by any means, electronic, mechanical, photocopying, recording or otherwise, without
the prior written permission of the publishers and copyright holders.

Conceived and produced by Berry & Co.
47 Crewys Road, London NW2 2AU
Designer: Debbie Mole
Illustrations: Kate Simunek

ISBN 978 1 84537 972 8

Senior Editor: Clare Johnson
Editorial Direction: Rosemary Wilkinson
Production: Hazel Kirkman

Reproduction by Pica Digital PTE Ltd, Singapore
Printed and bound by Times Offset (M) Sdn. Bhd., Malaysia

CONTENTS

INTRODUCTION

above: *The neatly rounded form of a small topiary box ball (Buxus sp.) provides the anchoring structure in a group of small plants on a table-top, under the rustic profusion of a clematis bower.*

opposite: *Formality rules in this smartly composed display of two bay standards (Laurus nobilis), under-planted with helxine (Solierolia solierolii) and connected by a window box planted up with a lavender (Lavandula dentata) standard and small box balls.*

THE ANCIENT ART OF TOPIARY – the geometric shaping of trees and shrubs - is a core design feature in classical gardens. Mention of topiary was made by Pliny the Elder (23-79AD) in Rome, who traced its invention to a friend of Julius Caesar, and many Roman estates featured clipped and trained plants of some description. The skill disappeared until medieval times when fruit trees were trained against the walls in enclosed gardens. But it was not until the Renaissance that topiary became hugely fashionable. The great Italian gardens produced parades of peacocks, bears and ships, holes were cut in hedges to frame breathtaking views and trees trained so that their branches intertwined (known as pleaching).

Demonstrating man's superiority over nature (the principle lying behind the French classical gardens of the 17th century), gardeners trained shrubs and trees into a whole host of symmetrical shapes, which were then used to create classical vistas. Elegant obelisks of clipped dark yew marked the entrance to a compartment of the garden, while beautifully laid out patterns in neat, small-leaved evergreens, such as box (*Buxus sempervirens*) were filled in with gravel, to provide an all-year-round pattern. This fashion then found favour in the great estates in England until, in the 18th century, the landscape gardener 'Capability' Brown swept away such conceits in favour of a naturalistic approach.

Since then topiary has waxed and waned in popularity, but it has always had its devotees. At its most complex, topiary can prove an extremely time-consuming art. The plants used for classical topiary are small-leaved and slow-growing, so it can take many years to achieve a large finished shape. Despite this, whole gardens have been based around topiary forms and shapes while others devote sections to virtuoso topiary skills – such as the famous chess set at Haseley Court in England. In yet others, a whimsical approach to topiary has informed

dianapolis-Marion County Public Library
w.imcpl.org
one:(317) 275-4410
lephone Renewal:(317) 269-5222

tle: Container topiary /
e: 08/16/10
em: 31973073395808

tal items checked out: 1

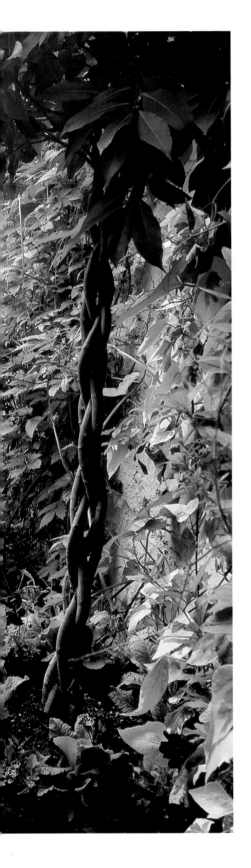

the design. At Marilyn Abbott's garden in Hampshire a small knot garden has been laid out with an "Alice in Wonderland" theme, complete with topiary characters drawn from the book.

For those with small gardens, even as small as a balcony or windowsill, the neatly clipped outlines of topiary can offer an air of elegance and formality. From little box balls in small terracotta pots ranged neatly on a window ledge to a pair of pompoms flanking a doorway, topiary in containers gives our houses and gardens the perfect finishing touch.

There are many purpose-made wire frames to be found for a wide variety of simple topiary shapes; these are used as an overall guide when trimming the shrub, making it easier to to produce a neat outline and relieving the need for any great design skill. A number of suppliers (see page 94) will furnish you with all manner of topiary frames from simple obelisks to fancy beasts, and from little teddy bears to elegant swans.

Topiary forms can be created just as easily in containers as they can in borders. You will, of course, need to feed and water the plants frequently, and clip and train them as assiduously as you would in the garden, but otherwise they do extremely well. One great advantage is that you can turn the pots so that any uneven growth caused by the shoots growing towards the light can be corrected.

Apart from the traditional shapes and the plants used to create them, there are novel forms of topiary with which to experiment. For the less patient, quick-growing ivy (*Hedera* sp.) presents an opportunity to create topiary shapes in months rather than years. For those prepared to exercise their imagination, almost any shape or idea is possible and there is a broad range of plants that you can employ (see Directory of Plants, pages 86-92).

left: *In this London garden, the clipped formality of box, much of it in containers, helps to contain and give shape to the planting. Large pots with underplanted box standards mark the entrance to the lawn, the path flanked on one side with a line of gaily striped containers of box balls.*

CHOOSING THE FORM that you wish your topiary to take is half the fun, since the choice before you is so varied. It makes sense, however, to opt for some of the simpler shapes until you are more familiar with the art and perhaps to create a couple of fast-growing topiaries from ivy alongside one or two more slow-growing traditional forms, so that you see a more rapid result for your labours.

It pays to consider where you are going to display your topiary before you start, so that its shape and size is appropriate for the setting you have in mind for it. If you want to create a matching pair of topiary containers for a doorstep, for example, then it might be better to choose a slender, elegant shape, such as a pyramid or perhaps a largish rectangle. You could create them from either box or privet (the latter is faster-growing than box but it will need more frequent clipping and shaping) or, for speed, from ivy.

In addition to the classic shapes, there are plenty of interesting shapes to choose from (see pages 24-47). You could even personalize your topiary by creating your own initials, for example.

If you want to create a topiary display, combining different shapes and sizes adds to the overall impact. Some of the most successful window box designs feature two small box balls flanking a slightly taller central pyramid, for example. By putting a pair of matching topiary window box displays on the sills of your windows, you help to emphasize the symmetrical nature of the architecture. Although it can look attractive to interplant the more sober topiary forms with flowering plants, you need to do this with care so that the simplicity of the topiary (its chief attribute) is not overwhelmed. Keep the subsidiary planting simple, ideally with a single colour theme, and avoid too many trailing plants.

right: *Many gardens are justifiably proud of their topiary creations. These beautifully clipped and maintained wedding cake tiers, peacocks and pyramids, on elegantly shaped bases, are brilliant examples of topiary art at its best.*

TOPIARY
techniques

Most fairly simple topiary shapes do not demand great skill to execute but you should make sure

that you maintain the plants in full vigour at all times for the topiaries to look their best. This chapter

explains how to choose and decorate the containers, the kind of topiary frames you can buy or make

to provide a guide for growing and training your plants, and how to tackle the basic cultivation,

including feeding, watering, general maintenance and propagation.

CONTAINER SHAPES AND SIZES

ONE THING IS CERTAIN: if you are going to the effort of creating your own topiary, you must take time and trouble choosing appropriate containers. The elegant form of the topiary shapes demands good-quality containers, and the overall size of the container must be appropriate for the size and scale of the topiary concerned.

There are various good quality materials to choose from, and many ready-made containers can be found in interesting shapes and sizes. The classic materials and shapes are often the most successful but some interesting new ideas have come into play in recent times, in particular the recycling of industrial materials, the minimal style of which seems to go very well with the stark, spare outlines of the topiary it contains.

When looking at proportion, bear in mind that the size of the container should, generally speaking, be one-third of the height of the finished topiary. This creates a reasonably attractive balance, but rules are made to be broken, and there may well be a case for surmounting a large container with quite a small topiary, although the opposite rarely applies: it usually looks slightly ludicrous, like a stout matron with very small feet.

terracotta

This is the most widely used, and probably most widely available material for containers. It has become increasingly popular over the years, and you can buy fine hand-thrown pots or machine-made mass-produced ones. Shapes and sizes vary from simple long Tom pots (with no lip) to more elaborate ones with a raised design, but generally speaking the plainer the pot, the more appropriate it is, in order to emphasize the architectural lines of the topiary itself. Hand-thrown pots have a wonderfully soft, delicate hue but the machine-made ones, while inexpensive, are disappointingly brash when new although they will weather in six months to a less intimidating colour. You can speed the process up by artificially ageing them (see page 16).

metal

The traditional metal containers were made of lead (difficult to lift, and now rather too valuable to entrust to the garden) but modern containers in anodized aluminium or matt steel can look very effective and would certainly look good on the windowsills, terrace or balcony of a modern-style apartment, for example. You can buy large planters – rectangular or square – or various rounded shapes, from cylinders to ellipses, which will give the topiary a modern touch. You can play around with the shapes of the pots and topiaries, putting a ball-shaped topiary in a square pot, and vice versa to add to the visual interest.

wood

There is a wide range of wooden tubs and window boxes available. The classic rectangular tub with finials at its four corners is known as the Versailles tub because it is a copy of the pots to be found at the famous French chateau garden of that name renowned for its parterres. Good-quality wood containers will last a long time, and their longevity will increase if you use a plastic liner inside the container. Don't forget to puncture its base to allow for drainage. Some funky modern containers have been created out of humble orange boxes, so nothing is sacred when it comes to making containers!

below (left): *Metal containers particularly suit geometric topiaries in modern settings.*

below (right): *Wooden containers – a Versailles tub made from bamboo and a slatted wooden trough are shown here – are always a popular choice for balconies and doorways.*

DECORATING CONTAINERS

IF YOU WISH, you can customize your containers in various ways to make them look more interesting. Anthony Noel, one of London's leading small-space garden designers, painted some of his in stripes (see page 27). In fact he painted so many that he said he eventually grew heartily sick of them, but a simple painted motif that is repeated on a row of small pots containing young box plants, awaiting their eventual transmogrification into topiary specimens, makes a feature out of your plant nursery. Unfussy designs suit the formal nature of topiary best. One simple method is to stencil a small motif onto each pot using gloss varnish only.

Modern machine-made terracotta pots often have a lip at the top of the pot, which could be painted in a contrasting colour or you can create your own band of colour on a flat-sided pot (see opposite).

If your pots, be they metal or terracotta, are too obviously new-looking, then consider distressing them to give them a more naturally antique appearance. Metal pots can be given a verdigris effect with separate coats of blue and green paint, stippled onto the surface and then sealed with acrylic varnish. For terracotta pots, use the simple ageing technique shown below.

How to age a terracotta pot

All you need to age a brand new terracotta pot in a matter of weeks (rather than the months it normally takes) is a carton of yogurt (use any out-of-date pots for the purposes of economy) and a small paintbrush.

1 Coat the container liberally with a thinnish layer of yogurt, revolving the pot on its base to do so.

2 Leave the container to dry for several hours and then pot up in the usual way. The effect above took three weeks to achieve.

How to decorate a terracotta pot

To create this simple but effective band of colour around the top of a long Tom terracotta container, all you need is a crayon, some architect's masking tape and a small pot of exterior gloss paint, in this case in forest green, and a paintbrush.

1 With a crayon, held between your thumb and forefinger and resting the tip of your finger on the pot edge, draw a line round the pot.

2 Apply architect's tape to the edge of the marked ring around the top of the pot. Press the tape down against the sides of the pot along the drawn line.

3 Load a fine brush and coat the edge of the pot neatly, taking care not to allow the paint to go over the edge of the rim.

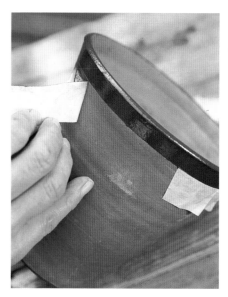

4 Allow the paint to dry thoroughly before carefully peeling off the architect's tape.

TOPIARY FRAMES

below: Made in galvanized wire, these are two of the simplest frames you could choose for your topiary, which can be made either from slow growing box or other small-leaved evergreen shrubs (see pages 88-92) or from quick-growing ivies for a much more speedy effect.

FRAMES ARE USED AS a guide for clipping and training topiary, and are generally simple wire constructions over which the plants can be trained. Some of the most popular shapes are rabbits, dogs, squirrels, chickens, cockerels, peacocks and swans, but all kinds of beasts, real or mythical, can be conjured up for the purpose. Frames for simple shapes, wider at the base than the top, are usually removed after clipping; those for the more elaborate shapes are left in situ.

Topiary shapes tend to go in and out of fashion. Teddy bears are increasingly popular, as are whimsical shapes, and you can also look around in junk yards and car boot sales for found objects, such as old car springs, around which to create modern topiary. Generally speaking, the less complex the outline, the quicker and easier it will be to create a realistic and satisfactory final effect.

The topiary does not always have to fill or cover the frame entirely, and some very attractive effects are created by allowing a few shoots of a pretty flowering climber to scramble over an intricately worked wire sphere (see page 58). To achieve a balanced appearance, make sure that you choose an appropriate sized container for the frame you have in mind.

making your own frames

You can make your own simple wire frames, if you wish, for which you will need heavy-gauge wire, either galvanized, copper or plastic-coated, a pair of wirecutters and a pair of pliers, as well as some reel wire for joining lengths of wire. To create a simple globe, for example, you can use suitable objects, such as old flower pots, around which you can bend the wire into a simple circle. Two circles of the same size with a small "tail" wire at the join complete the structure. Chicken wire can be used to cover the shape if you then want to make a fully covered globe (see page 62). Remember to use gloves when cutting chicken wire – it is very sharp.

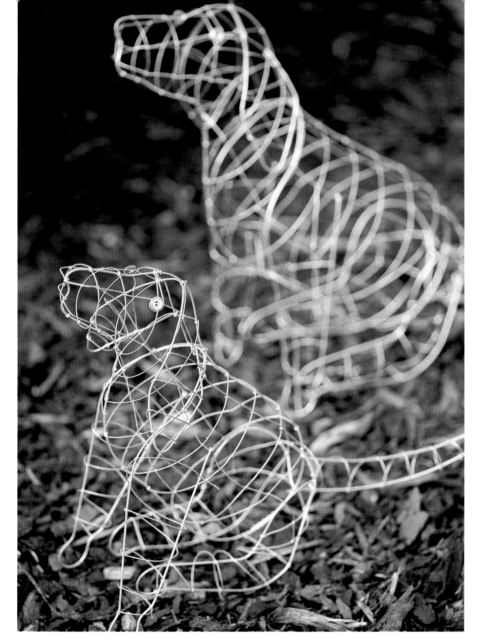

left: *Some topiary frames are so beautifully constructed that they make sculptural elements in their own right. These two dogs are almost too good to serve as growing guides!*

below: *Animal and bird shapes are popular and good fun to grow. Smaller shapes will achieve their required forms quite rapidly if you choose plants to train that are already well grown.*

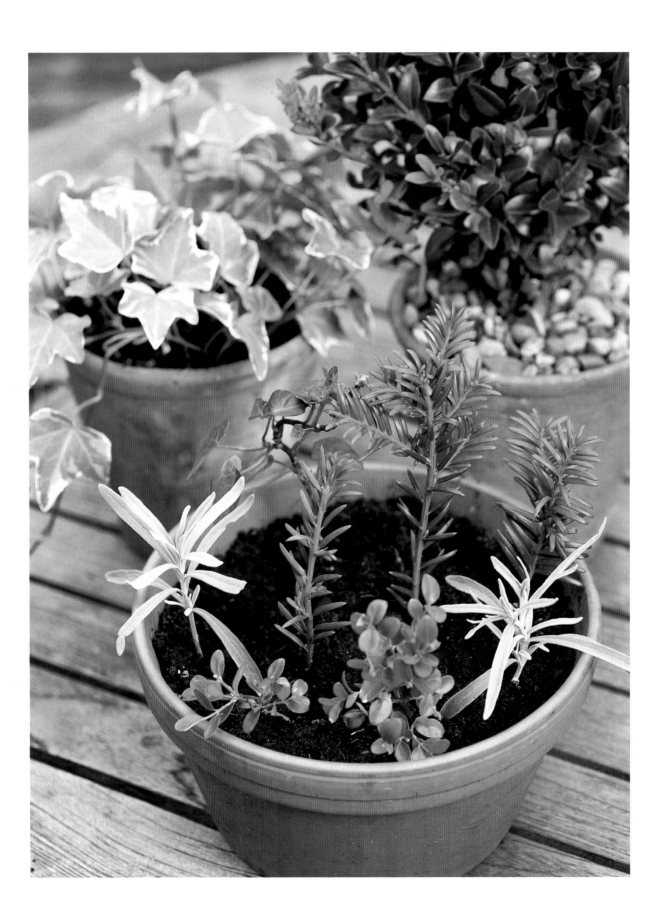

BASIC CULTIVATION

YOUNG PLANTS FOR TOPIARY can be purchased from a garden centre or nursery. Your choice of plant will be determined by the style of topiary you have in mind. Neatly clipped forms require plants with small evergreen leaves, standards require trees, shrubs or perennials with a woody stem, and false topiary needs quick-growing climbing plants.

Remember that all plants need adequate light, although some, such as ivy, will cope with shade levels well below the norm. Remember to position those plants that need good sun in the right place (see individual plant entries on pages 88-92 for information on appropriate conditions).

equipment

Apart from the basic pots and multipurpose potting compost, you need very little basic equipment for topiary apart from a pair of good-quality secateurs, a pair of shears and a pair of garden scissors. You will also need a watering can.

planting

When you plant, you must use clean pots large enough to give the rootball space to grow (a diameter 8cm/3in larger than that of the rootball is the norm). The pot must have adequate drainage, and, if you use some kind of found object, such as a metal bucket, as a container, remember to drill holes in the base for this purpose. The holes should then be covered with some shards of broken pots, or large pebbles, so that they do not become blocked with compost and so that the compost does not wash away when the plant is watered.

To plant up, fill the pot one-third full with a multipurpose potting compost, spread out the roots of the plant to be potted and position it so that the crown of the plant (where the stem starts) is level with the top of the soil (about 2.5cm/1in below the surface of the pot to allow room for watering). Firm the compost down well with the heels of your hands. Water thoroughly and add a mulch to the surface (pebbles, cocoa shells or mussel shells are all ideal) to prevent future moisture loss.

opposite: *A selection of evergreen cuttings, including lavender, box, yew and rosemary. If you take a couple of cuttings, you stand a better chance that at least one will grow on to maturity. Most cuttings take about 10–12 weeks to root, during which time they must be kept moist but not waterlogged.*

above: *A mulch of gravel over the surface of the compost will help to reduce moisture loss and prevent weeds growing.*

above (left): *Fertilizers often need to be mixed with water before use. For the best results, take care to dilute the feed according to the manufacturers' instructions.*

above (centre): *Water plants regularly to ensure that they do not become stressed, aiming to keep the compost moist at all times.*

above (right): *To ensure you clip topiary evenly on all sides, you can use a metal or wood frame to the shape required, clipping only those shoots that protrude beyond its outline.*

feeding

This is an essential element in creating container topiaries, since the aim is to get the plants growing as vigorously as possible. Bear in mind that the nutrient content of the compost you used for planting up lasts for only a few weeks. After that you will need to feed the plant roughly once a month while it is actively growing (spring to autumn). In order for the plant to be able to take up the nutrients the compost must be moist, so regular watering is also essential.

There are various kinds of feed you can use from a simple dressing of home-made compost (well-rotted vegetable matter) to purpose-bought fertilizers that are specially formulated for certain plants. Quick pick-me-ups can be provided with foliar feeds, which are sprayed direct onto the leaves, and you can also buy slow-release fertilizer granules which cut down on the frequency of feeding.

watering

Some plants are more drought resistant than others. Lavender and rosemary, both useful plants for training into standards, can cope without water for longer than many other plants, and ivy (the most popular quick topiary plant) also copes well without much water, but none will grow as fast as a result.

You can feel whether the plant needs watering by familiarizing yourself with the weight of the container. A recently watered container is surprisingly heavy; one that is suffering from drought surprisingly light. (You can buy moisture-gauge sticks that give a reading that indicates whether watering is necessary.) If you have let the container dry out, then plunge the pot and the plant within it into a bucket of water and leave it there until the bubbles stop rising. Most of us water too little but overwatering can also be a problem. The compost should be moist not constantly soaking wet.

general maintenance

The techniques for clipping and shaping the plants are covered in the individual entries. However, you will also need to take care of your plants in the winter if they are tender (see Directory of Plants, pages 88-92) and if you live in a cold climate. Those that are marginally frost tolerant can have the pots wrapped in hessian or bubble wrap in the coldest months. Tender plants will have to brought indoors once the frosts start.

Keep any tools you use for clipping and pruning sharp and well oiled, as torn cuts are likely to encourage diseases, apart from making the plants themselves look untidy. There are, unhappily, quite a few pests and diseases which may attack your handiwork. You can guard against them, to some extent, by ensuring that you keep the plants well watered and well fed, and that they are in conditions where the air can circulate reasonably well.

simple propagation

Although container-grown plants are expensive to buy, many of them can be raised relatively easily from cuttings – small sideshoots removed from the parent plant. Box generally grows very easily from cuttings, so you can raise a whole forest of topiary plants, if you have the space. Information on the various types of cutting appropriate for different topiary plants, and when to take them, are given in the individual plant entries on pages 88-92.

How to take a box cutting

Box is one of the principal topiary plants and one of the easiest to propagate. It will grow well from a small sideshoot about 10cm (4in) removed from a stouter stem with a small heel of bark. Prepare a small pot filling it with a mixture of potting compost and a handful of grit.

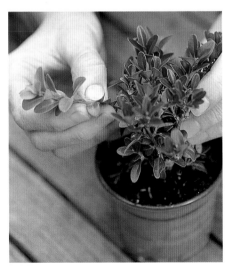

1 Remove a suitably sized cutting from the parent plant, pulling away a small heel of bark from the stem as you do so.

2 Insert the cutting into the compost to a depth of an inch or so. Water the pot and keep moist (cover it with clear plastic to conserve moisture).

SIMPLE
shapes

Some of the most effective, and the most popular, topiary shapes are those based on simple geometry – balls, cubes and pyramids. This chapter shows you how to create these basic shapes from small-leaved evergreens, such as box, using well-grown young plants. If you create a matching pair, they are ideal for framing a doorway, for example. Equally, use a line of small topiary balls to define a path or a flight of steps.

opposite: *A group of box balls in striking striped pots, flanked by two neat cubes, make an attractive formal display in front of a wall-mounted water feature. The symmetrical nature of the display gives it an elegant, classical feel.*

SOMETIMES THE SIMPLEST and easiest shapes – geometric cubes, balls and pyramids – are the most effective. However, they will need to be properly cared for and well trimmed to look good, as any browned or wayward shoots will be particularly obvious.

The classic topiary plants are the best choice for simple shapes: box, privet and yew are ideal for balls, squares or pyramids, as the small dark evergreen leaves produce a neat, clear outline.

Some people prefer to use a frame as a cutting guide when trimming topiary, but in fact you can often manage to trim small, simple topiary shapes by eye. However, you need to work carefully, in stages, as it is only too easy to keep snipping bits off until very little remains! When trimming these shapes, you need to turn the topiary as you work so that the result is even. If you are trimming several topiaries that will be displayed together, it is helpful to use a frame to ensure that they all achieve the same size and form.

The small simple shapes have the greatest impact when displayed in groups, either using repeating motifs of the same shape, or combining them in symmetrical formations, such as a pyramid flanked by two balls, or perhaps four square topiaries to mark the intersection between two paths.

If you wish, you can use a central small topiary shape to provide the mainstay of a window box, or pair of window boxes, with softer planting that is renewed seasonally on either side of this all-year-round foliage feature. Small shapes look equally good lined up in rows on a window sill, or as a feature pair on top of gateposts, or positioned either side of the front or back door.

Make sure when creating grouped displays that you use matching materials for the containers, either by opting for one specific type, such as metal or terracotta, or by painting more disparate pots in the same colour, or in a range of toning colours. This is particularly important if you are grouping together a range of shapes to add some sense of unity to the display. Be careful, too, that the container size suits the shape and scale of the topiary.

SIMPLE TOPIARY CUBE

THIS IS ONE of the least complex topiary shapes, but its very simplicity can be slightly deceptive, since it relies on precise trimming to look good, and very dense foliage, achieved by frequent trimming over several seasons. The best plants to choose are box, in one of its many forms, privet (*Ligustrum* sp.) and yew (*Taxus baccata*), as these will all create the necessary dense foliage. Although you can trim the shape by eye, you will find it easier if you use a cube-shaped guide to ensure that the sides of the cube are as straight as possible.

Pairs of cubes can be used to flank displays of more elaborate topiaries. Make sure the dimensions of the cubes suit the scale of the other plants in the display. With their crisp outline, modern, minimalist containers suit them best.

opposite: *This neat box cube has been given a contemporary appearance with a container made from a recycled packing case, but a rectangular terracotta or stainless steel container would look more formal.*

How to create a topiary cube

To make a cube roughly 30cm (12in) square, you need to grow the topiary (or buy a suitable plant) that has already reached roughly this height. A simple metal cutting guide to the size required will help to ensure an even shape. Plant up in a container at least as wide as the proposed dimensions of the cube. The topiary will need to be clipped twice yearly in late spring and late summer until the shape is achieved.

1 Position the cutting guide over the plant. Pinch out the topmost growth at the required height, and then trim all the sideshoots by a couple of centimetres.

2 As the plant begins to bush out, remove any straggling shoots that protrude beyond the cutting frame. Supply regular doses of seaweed based fertilizer to encourage growth.

3 Then trim twice yearly. By the second season, the shape should be more or less achieved. Clipping in subsequent seasons will help to create a more dense shape.

SIMPLE TOPIARY PYRAMID

THIS PARTICULAR SHAPE makes an extremely effective topiary, and is among the most popular, being both elegant and eye-catching. You can make topiary pyramids based either on a traditional 3-sided pyramid or on a cone. There are a number of evergreens that lend themselves to this form, including bay *(Laurus nobilis)*, privet, yew, and cypress *(Chamaecyparis sp.)* as well as the ubiquitous box *(Buxus sp.)* in its many species and varieties.

The rounded pyramid is the easier of the two shapes to construct and follow and can be cut by eye once the basic pyramid shape is achieved. A three-sided cone is best cut with a frame, to ensure that each "face" of the cone is evenly shaped and sized.

How to create a topiary pyramid

Once you have grown on a plant to roughly the right height and shape (use a bought frame to create the approximate pyramid shape), you can then clip it more tightly to its final shape. It will need to be trimmed twice a season, in late spring and summer, to keep its outline.

1 When the plant has grown on to the roughly the right height, and you have clipped it to an approximate pyramid shape, nip out the tip of the leading shoot.

2 Start to make the first cut, working up from the base of the pyramid to the top, taking a small section of the plant and cutting back the shoots by the most recent growth.

3 Work your way around the pyramid a section at a time, and then finally clip it lightly all over once you have succeeded in achieving a well-balanced outline.

opposite (top): *A young topiary pyramid. As you clip it each season, it will gradually create a more dense shape, similar to the one shown left.*

left: *This well-clipped box pyramid has a good, neat shape, achieved by regular trimming. The metal container, and the gravel mulch used to cover the compost, add a modern twist to a classical design.*

SIMPLE TOPIARY BALLS

above: *A series of small topiary balls, each in a hand-painted striped container, are ideal for edging a path or patio.*

THESE SIMPLE LITTLE BALLS are relatively easy to create. Being small, they do not take years to grow into the required form. To achieve more impact, grow several and line them up in a row on a windowsill or to flank a path, or put them in pairs on a flight of steps. You can either buy a circular frame to act as a clipping guide or you can take your courage in your own hands and clip them freeform. Achieving an identical result for several balls may be more difficult and is best done using a frame.

The best plant to use for the smallest spheres is the very small leaved box (*Buxus microphylla*). Larger ones could be created from privet (both golden- and green-leaved forms). For rapid results, go for the false topiary globe in ivy shown on page 62.

To add interest to a series of box balls, consider painting or decorating the containers in a smart but suitably elegant design, such as the stripes shown here or with a glazed motif stencilled onto the pot and simply varnished.

How to create a simple box ball

You will need a plant grown on to a height a few centimetres taller than the eventual height of the sphere, as this will create the shape much more quickly and will be easier to trim.

1 Grow the box plant on, clipping it into a rough ball shape until it is about 5cm (2in) more than the circumference required.

2 Tie a piece of tape around the widest part of the plant to the measurement required. Start to trim around this guide.

3 Then trim the plant in sections, starting with the top centre. Clip the top sections and then clip from the centre to the base.

FANCY

shapes

The range of topiary shapes you can create is limited only by your determination. Those shown on the following pages are all popular ones to create, and within the grasp of any amateur topiary fancier. Creating matched pairs of more elaborate shapes is rather more difficult since it is hard to be absolutely precise with measurements. Shapes in this section include spirals, pompoms, a heart, a hen and a peacock.

IF YOU HAVE caught the topiary bug, you will want to experiment with ever more fanciful shapes to show off your new-found skills. Some of the most popular are tiered pompoms with a length of clear stem in between each pompom. They vary in form from two simple equal-sized pompoms, stacked one on top of the other, to more elaborate "wedding cake" tiers.

Another popular fancy shape is the spiral, usually with four or five "twists". The proportions of the twists are a matter of choice: some have a more serpentine shape with wider cuts, in others a more densely formed spiral shape is preferred. The former creates a more vigorous, dynamic feel to the topiary; the latter is more geometric in shape, and looks more formal.

Apart from the selection shown on the following pages, you can make your own composite shapes. You could make a square based topiary with a pompom shape directly on top of it, for example, rather than leaving the usual length of clear stem.

It is best to display these fancy shapes in symmetrical pairs, or in company with other simple topiary shapes, which provide an attractive foil for your more elaborate handiwork.

The smallest leaved evergreens will give the neatest shape so, for fancy shapes, pick plants carefully that will show off the form to best effect. Box, yew and privet are the most commonly used for spirals and cakestand-type pompoms, but holly makes successful round ball-shaped pompoms.

Animal and bird shapes have long been popular for topiary. The easier ones to create are those with a simple body structure (such as a hen, peacock or swan) which is clipped from the main growth of the plant. Top- and sideshoots are then trained to create the head and beak at one end and the tail feathers at the other. Of the fancy shapes, the heart (on page 46) is popular and relatively easy to create.

below: *This terrace has an attractive mixture of topiary shapes, including pompoms and standards. Varying the shapes and plants helps to create a more lively-looking display.*

TOPIARY SPIRALS

FOR A MORE ELABORATE variation on the basic topiary pyramid or cone, you can create the illusion of a spiral-grown plant by cutting and trimming a pre-grown topiary pyramid (see page 30) to the appropriate shape. You will either have to grow the topiary yourself to approximately the right height and form, and then clip it into shape or you can buy a ready-made topiary pyramid. A healthy plant with even growth on all sides is a prerequisite for this shape. You need to give the topiary a quarter turn every couple of months to ensure the shoots grow evenly on all sides. Once the topiary is clipped into the right form, it will need trimming with shears twice a year in summer to keep its shape.

opposite: *A handsome box spiral forms the centrepiece in this topiary display, flanked by pompoms and a simple box ball. It often pays to create one of the topiaries from a variegated form, to give a lighter effect.*

How to create a box spiral

Apart from a topiary pyramid that has one strong central stem, you will need a length of wide tape, sufficient to wind around the proposed topiary pyramid as a cutting guide. You will also need a couple of clips (bulldog ones are ideal) to hold the tape in place at the top and base of the pyramid.

1 When the topiary has reached the appropriate size, nip out the leading (topmost) shoot to prevent further growth. Trim the new growth to make an even conical shape (see page 30).

2 Attach the tape to the base of the pyramid and wind it around, at evenly spaced intervals, from the base to the tip. Start to clip away the foliage either side of the tape.

3 Once you have clipped the appropriate rough spiral shape you can remove the tape. Trim the shape to the desired depth (right back to the central stem for a more defined spiral).

TOPIARY POMPOMS

opposite: *The charm of these topiary pompoms lies in the way in which they have been grouped. Staggering the heights of topiaries is one way to ensure that they are seen to advantage.*

THE EASIEST WAY to create a topiary pompom is to cut the shape out from an already established topiary cone, in much the same way that the topiary spiral is created. If you do this, you are better able to achieve a really neat shape. If you continue to close clip the pompoms, they will bush out and become more dense, their form gradually improving over a couple of seasons.

The style of pompom can vary. Some are made with evenly spaced tiers, diminishing in size towards the top. Others consists of a round ball shape at the base with a clear stem, crowned by a much smaller pompom. You could also combine one of the fancy shapes with a pompom base.

How to create a topiary pompom

First, create a roughly cut topiary pyramid (see page 30) out of the chosen plant material, ideally an evergreen with neat, small leaves and a strong central stem. Decide on the number and thickness of the pompoms you wish to create. They look best with a graduated appearance, the largest at the base. You will need a couple of lengths of tape.

1 Firstly, mark off the areas that need to be cut back, and wind tape around the plant to form a cutting guide. Nip out the leading shoot of the plant to stop further growth.

2 Using secateurs, start to clip out the branches between the proposed pompoms, cutting right back to the central stem.

3 Then start to shape the pompoms (in the same way as the box ball on page 33), starting at the base and working up to the topmost pompom.

ANIMAL SHAPES

opposite: *This little topiary hen is still growing into its shape. In another season or so, the head and tail of the bird will have grown to fill out the frame, as will the body. Frequent clipping will give it a more dense appearance.*

WITHOUT DOUBT, these are the most fun to create and surprisingly effective results can be achieved in a relatively short space of time. The quickest shapes to produce are those which are relatively simple and which follow the normal growth patterns of the chosen plant. Those in which individual branches have to be trained to produce more elongated elements will take much longer, although they are not necessarily more difficult.

Hens and peacocks are popular shapes simply because they work so well – a topiary hen is shown below and a topiary peacock overleaf. A purpose-made wire frame is essential, and most good topiary suppliers stock them (see page 94).

How to create a topiary hen

You will need to purchase an appropriate wire frame to the required size. You can start this topiary with any sized plant, but if you buy one that is already well grown, you will achieve the shape in much less time. You will need to trim it twice each season until the required shape is achieved.

1 Plant up the chosen plant, grown to at least as tall as the basic shape, in the container of your choice. Position the cutting guide over the plant.

2 Divide the foliage into three parts, one each for the tail, head and back of the hen. Tie in loosely using garden ties.

3 Clip the centre part of the plant level with the hen's back and trim any straggling shoots at the tail and head end that protrude beyond the frame. Then clip twice annually, using the frame as a guide until the frame is covered.

above and right:

A topiary peacock makes an attractive display. The little peacock (above) made from box is still growing into its frame; the peacock (right) from boxleaved honeysuckle (Lonicera nitida) has already done so, with its leading shoots forming the distinctive peacock's crown, and it is now ready for a final clip.

For a cockerel, you will need to allow one clump of shoots to grow on, so that it bushes out to make the tail feathers. This is also true of the peacock shown on this page, in which the shoots for the tail feathers are allowed to grow on and trained into a fan shape.

More elaborate animals shapes can be created simply by tying in sections of the plant while training others to extend in the direction required, often by using a training cane to which the extending shoots are attached. Animal shapes, such as dogs in which the base consists of four legs are best created using an appropriate number of plants. For a simple dog shape in which the two front and two back legs are blocked, two plants will do. For a more clearly four-legged shape you will need four plants. The plants are then trained in exactly the same way as the hen (see previous page).

How to make a topiary peacock

It is easiest to make this particular shape if you start with a well-grown bushy plant with an adequate number of good branches to form the fanned-out tail. You can then use the peacock-shaped frame as a cutting guide. To encourage the plant to grow rapidly, use a good seaweed-based feed once a month in the growing season.

1 Plant up as for the hen (see page 42), and insert the frame. Then divide the plant into three equal parts, one for the head, one for the back and one for the tail.

2 Clip the central part of the peacock back to the outline frame. Clip any protruding branches back from the tail and head ends of the peacock.

3 Keep clipping the body of the peacock back by roughly 10cm (4in) each year, but clip the tail feathers only by a couple of centimetres. By the third year, this should be fully grown and densely covered.

TOPIARY HEART

THERE ARE A NUMBER of ways that you can go about making a topiary heart. The one shown right and below is a traditional box heart, shaped using a simple single wire frame, but you can, if you wish, opt for one of the quick topiary techniques and make a similar shape very easily using ivy instead of box, tying in the new shoots as they grow as you would for the ivy globe or sphere (see pages 62–3).

If you prefer a more dense effect, you can purchase or make a heart-shaped frame with a 3D appearance (it will have a couple of additional supporting wires running from the top of the heart to the base, and around the centre of the structure). You can then cover it with chicken wire, stuff it with moss and grow ivy over the whole structure to form a completely dense shape.

If the shape stands quite proud of the container, it pays to mulch the container, to prevent weeds growing and conserve moisture, and to give it a smarter appearance.

opposite: This small topiary heart, measuring some 45cm (18in) in height, has been made out of box, trained around a galvanized wire frame.

How to make a topiary heart

You will need a simple heart-shaped wire frame. You can buy one readymade or you can make it by inserting a nail on a board. Use this as the centre point for the V-shape of the heart and then shape the heart by hand, twisting the wires into a tail to form a support. A well-grown box plant that will divide easily into two sections is needed as well.

1 Plant up the box plant in the usual way, and insert the frame into the pot, ensuring it is firmly anchored in the compost. Divide the plant into two halves, tying each half into either side of the frame.

2 Keep tying the leading shoots into the wire frame. When they are long enough to reach the V of the heart, cross the shoots over and tie them together loosely.

3 Clip the shape twice a season. It will gradually thicken to cover the frame completely.

TOPIARY
standards

Standards – neat balls of flowers or foliage on top of a clear stem – make an interesting variation on topiary. Many different plants can be trained into this shape, from roses to holly. They can be used to add height to a group of plants in containers, or to add interest to display of geometric topiaries. In matched pairs, they are the ideal plants for a doorstep, taking up very little of the available space. You can underplant them with seasonal flowers, such as spring bulbs or summer bedding.

above: *Planting up a small standard in a large pot leaves room to grow flowering plants below. The display can be changed each season (pansies in winter, tulips in spring, busy lizzies in summer, and cyclamens in winter) while the foliage standard provides the central architectural feature.*

opposite: *Foliage standards are the ideal choice to create a feature display on a step, taking up very little of the available space. Their neat form provides all-year-round interest, the architecture providing the ideal background.*

TRAINING PLANTS INTO STANDARDS, where a straight stem is surmounted with a bushy head of leaves, flowers or fruit, rather like a lollipop, is now an increasingly fashionable design idea. The concept is not new: it reached its heyday in Victorian times. At first, this did not find favour with gardeners who felt the practice went against the natural order but the popularity of standard roses helped to make the technique more acceptable. To this day, most people are familiar with the concept of pruning roses into standards, but perhaps less so with the notion that almost any shrub with a strong stem can be trained into a similar lollipop shape.

The plants that lend themselves most readily to this treatment are certain highly floriferous shrubs, such as roses and fuchsias, so that the mop-head atop the stem is a ball of blooms, and small-leaved evergreens, whose glossy foliage can be clipped to make a neat ball. Good candidates here are bay, myrtle and viburnum (which have the bonus of scented flowers as well as attractive foliage), but there is a wide range to choose from (see pages 88-92).

While most standards are created from the simple expedient of removing the lower side shoots until a clear stem of the appropriate height is formed, and then removing the growing point so that the mop head is created at the top, grafting enables you to join species together to create something altogether more unusual (see pages 56-7). This technique reached its height in the mid-19th century with some very bizarre creations, including one display where weeping beeches were grafted onto mature cedars. Those of us limited to small-space gardening, and with containers as our only growing space, are unlikely to echo these particular follies, but the technique of grafting is not difficult and the joining together of two plants with different characteristics and attributes does widen the design scope.

right: *A fuchsia standard makes an attractive summer display for a doorway. If you wish to prolong the interest, plant the container with smaller flowering plants during the different seasons.*

opposite: *Among the many plants that respond well to training into standards are woody herbs such as lavender and rosemary. Being evergreen, they provide interest all year with the bonus of attractive flowers in summer.*

FLOWERING STANDARDS

THERE IS A SURPRISINGLY wide range of flowering plants that you can train into a standard shape. By far the greatest number are shrubs, but you can also use some perennials, with the help of a stake to which the stem is tied, and some climbers, which will also need staking.

The most popular plants are roses and fuchsias, but there are some less usual shrubs and climbers that you can try. Viburnum, for example, makes a dense head of foliage with the bonus of white flowers (some species and hybrids are scented) from early to late spring. Herbs, too, can be trained into standards, in particular, rosemary and lavender.

How to create a flowering standard

It is important to bear in mind that the plant will be encouraged to bush out only if the leading shoot (once it attains the required height) is pinched out (the topmost leaves removed). This encourages the remaining shoots to grow, creating the requisite mop-head. While you need to remove branches to create the clear stem, you must leave small sideshoots in place, to give the plant the opportunity to take up food.

1 Plant up an appropriately sized young plant with a strong central growing stem in the chosen container. Remove side branches, but leave some small sideshoots in place.

2 Pinch out the growing point of the central stem and the sideshoots and leave topmost shoots unpruned. Tie in the main stem of weaker-stemmed plants to a central stake.

3 Continue to pinch out the leading shoot. Prune back the topmost sideshoots by about one third just after flowering. They will bush out to form a mop-head top.

FOLIAGE STANDARDS

FOR ARCHITECTURAL EFFECT, you can opt for standards created from ever-green shrubs. Trained into the typical ball shape, they look good all year round. Bay, a handsome evergreen with aromatic leaves, is one of the best known and makes a singularly elegant shape, often used as classic doorway sentinels. Bay was thought to guard the house against bad spirits.

Other good shrubs for training into evergreen standards are myrtle with the bonus of scented white flowers and holly (*Ilex* sp). There are many hollies to choose from, from the smallest spiny leaved dark green ones to more glamorous golden- or silver-variegated forms (see page 89). Their densely packed branches of foliage make neat mop-heads of leaves, often with the bonus of shiny red berries. Citrus trees, with their neat, glossy, evergreen leaves, also make good subjects for clipping into standards but will need winter protection in colder areas.

PROTECTING STAKES

If you are using canes to support a standard while the stem is maturing, remember to cover the tip. Gardeners are particularly prone to eye accidents from uncovered stakes!

How to create a foliage standard

Choose a plant with a well-formed central stem at least 90cm (3ft) tall. For a standard of this height you will need a container roughly 30cm (12in) in diameter. Plants with weak stems will need staking, for which you will need a stout cane and some garden ties.

1 Plant up in the usual way and stake the central stem to a support, tying in at intervals with plastic garden ties. Once the stem is strong enough, the stake can be removed.

2 Remove any large side shoots from the main stem up to 30cm (12in) below the top of the plant. When the plant reaches the chosen height, pinch out the leading shoot.

3 The following season pinch out the leading shoot again, and keep trimming the side shoots just below it to encourage them to bush out and grow more vigorously. Clip the shape into the form of a ball.

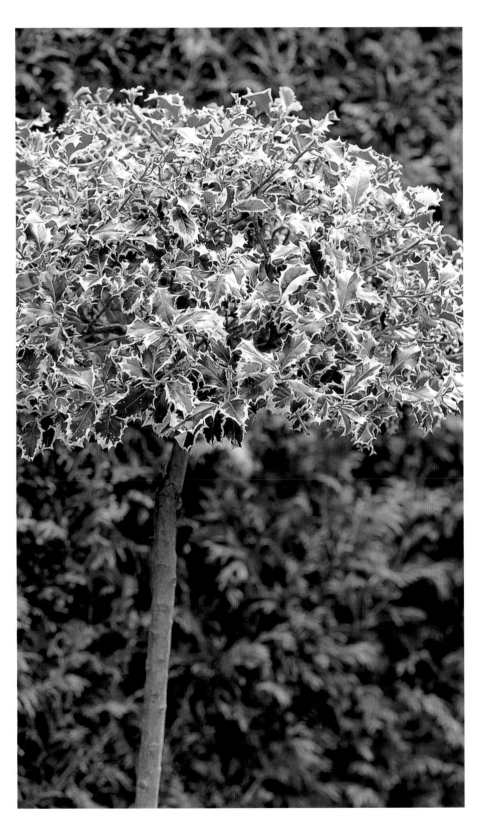

left: *This variegated holly standard has made a handsome ball of foliage on top of a strong clear stem. Hollies with gold- or silver-edged leaves are a good choice, as the paler coloured margins to the leaves help to create a lighter effect.*

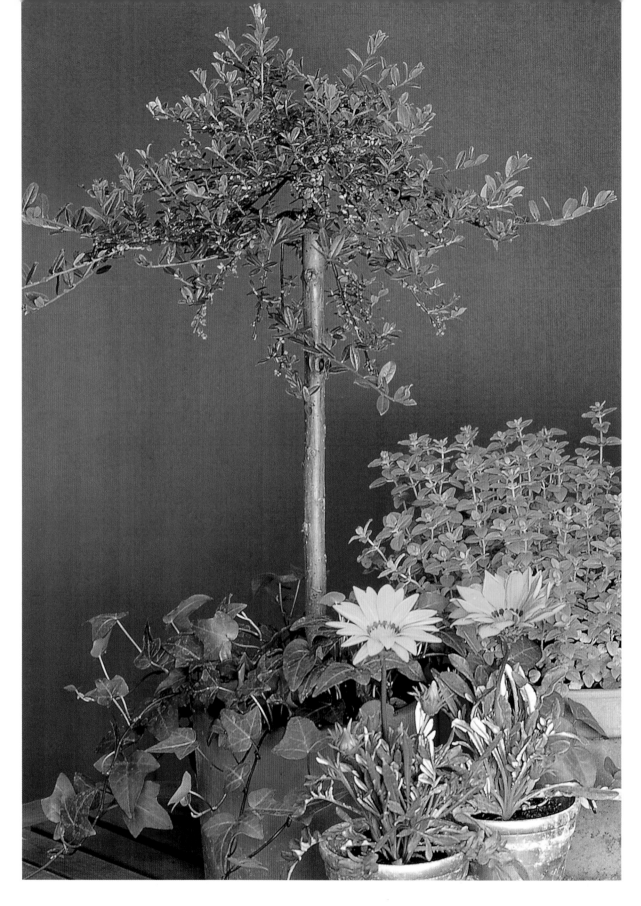

a b o v e : *This little weeping willow has been created from a low-growing willow (*Salix x caprea*) grafted onto a taller growing willow main stem. It bears attractive catkins in spring.*

GRAFTED STANDARDS

WHERE YOU WANT to obtain a particular mophead effect, but the plant itself will not produce the requisite clear stem, you can graft two plants together. The plant that provides the base must have a naturally straight, strong stem, obtained from one central leader. Once it has reached the required size, it is trimmed back and the stem of the new plant is then grafted onto the uppermost part of the stem of the base plant. There are a number of different grafting methods that can be employed, but the one shown below is easy enough for an amateur to copy. Among the many plants that are grafted are roses, in which a more vigorous rootstock is used for the supporting stem and a very floriferous rose for the mophead. An unusual combination is a small willow standard, in which a more vigorous rootstock provides the support for a prettily weeping variety.

GRAFT UNION

This close-up shows the graft union between the two plants that have been joined together to make the standard willow.

How to create a grafted standard

By cutting into the bark, you expose the layer known as the cambium whose healing properties allow the stock and the scion (the plant being grafted onto the stock) to knit together.

1 Make a single upward slanting cut about 5cm (2in) long at the base of the top section of the plant, and a matching cut on the bottom section of the rootstock.

2 Position the two cut surfaces of each plant so that they match. Once they are in position, bind them with an elastic band.

3 Put the newly grafted plant into a pot of compost, and keep the grafted area moist (cover it with a plastic bag) until the wound heals.

QUICK
topiary

In addition to classical topiary, you can create imaginative topiaries from quick-growing plants, such as ivies and other fast-growing climbers, or from pots of flowering plants, such as pansies, scillas and small tulips, built up to echo geometric topiary forms. You can even trim grass to make topiary style features, such as benches or chairs.

opposite: *This tulip tower has been built up using a series of stacking pots (see the pansies on page 68 for instructions). The effect is similar to topiary, but obviously short-lived. It can make a splendid feature for a few weeks, and is a great feature or talking point for a special occasion.*

FOR THOSE OF US who are too impatient to wait several seasons for slow-growing plants like box to grow into the required topiary shape, there are other options. Quick-growing climbers, such as ivies, can be trained to cover traditional topiary wire forms, such as pyramids, spheres and spirals, or some of the more fantastic ones, such as beasts and birds. Another alternative is to use climbers to partially clothe an attractive wire frame, which creates an almost sculptural effect (see page 58).

Fast-growing climbers will do their stuff surprisingly quickly, covering a small frame in one growing season, and a larger one in a couple of seasons. You will need to pay particular attention to the way you care for this more unusual type of topiary, since the key element is that it looks good and retains its shape, an essential ingredient in the overall design.

In addition to the classic forms of topiary, there are inventive and original designs you can employ, using fast-growing climbers, for example, or structures that produce a topiary-like shape using flowers. These novelty shapes can vary from topiary chairs and benches, created from neatly clipped grasses and herbs, to slender columns of flowers, using pansies or tulips, for example, built up in a series of containers to form pyramids or cylinders. The aim with all of these designs is to produce a formal effect and a neat, even appearance, so they need to be constructed carefully. While foliage topiaries are evergreen, creating all-year-round features in the garden, a flowering topiary has a relatively short season of interest, but is a showstopper while in flower.

By choosing more unusual plants or styles for topiary, you can add life and interest to the garden planting, and an element of fun. Although the origins of topiary are classical, it has always offered its practitioners an opportunity to experiment and release their creativity, as the herds of topiary sheep or the hunt in full cry in some of the great country house gardens attest.

Trained trees and shrubs (kept to miniature sizes by ensuring the roots do not grow), known as bonsai, are another type of topiary. An art form in Japan, these small formal, clipped plants make attractive features for table tops on balconies and can be bought ready grown in many good garden centres, the only requirement then being to maintain them in good order with regular clipping.

FALSE TOPIARY GLOBE

YOU CAN EITHER create a open frame for this little topiary ornament, growing the ivy only over the uprights (opposite) or you can cover the entire structure (left) with chicken wire to create the sphere, left. Much depends on the setting you have in mind for it. Whichever you choose, they look good as a matching pair, framing a trough of flowering plants for example, or you could set them on a pedestal, or atop a pair of gateposts.

The best ivies to use for smaller-size frames are those with small, neat leaves, such as 'Pedata' or 'Conglomerata' as the scale is better suited to the frame. Equally good are the variegated ivies such as 'Goldheart', which produce an attractive, ethereal effect.

above: *This ivy sphere was made using a chicken-wire and moss form.*

The size and shape of the globe will determine how many ivy plants you need to cover it. If you are aiming to cover the entire globe, you will get the best coverage using around six plants for a sphere roughly 60cm (24in) in diameter. For the small open globe shown here, four plants were sufficient.

How to create an ivy globe

For the ivy globe, opposite, you will need some young ivy plants (around 15cm/6in tall - ivy grows very quickly from cuttings) and a globe frame made from two circles of wire. If you wish to create the dense ivy sphere (above), then add horizontal wires on which to train the shoots.

1 Select a suitably sized container that balances the size and shape of the globe. Crock the pot, and fill with growing medium two-thirds full. Plant the ivy plants around the perimeter of the pot.

2 Insert the globe frame and start to train the shoots up each upright, twisting them around the wire supports. If necessary, tie the shoots in loosely with plant ties.

3 As the stems grow, carry on twisting them around the frame. Once they have covered the frame fully, you can snip off the growing points, and trim the ivy at intervals with secateurs to keep it in shape.

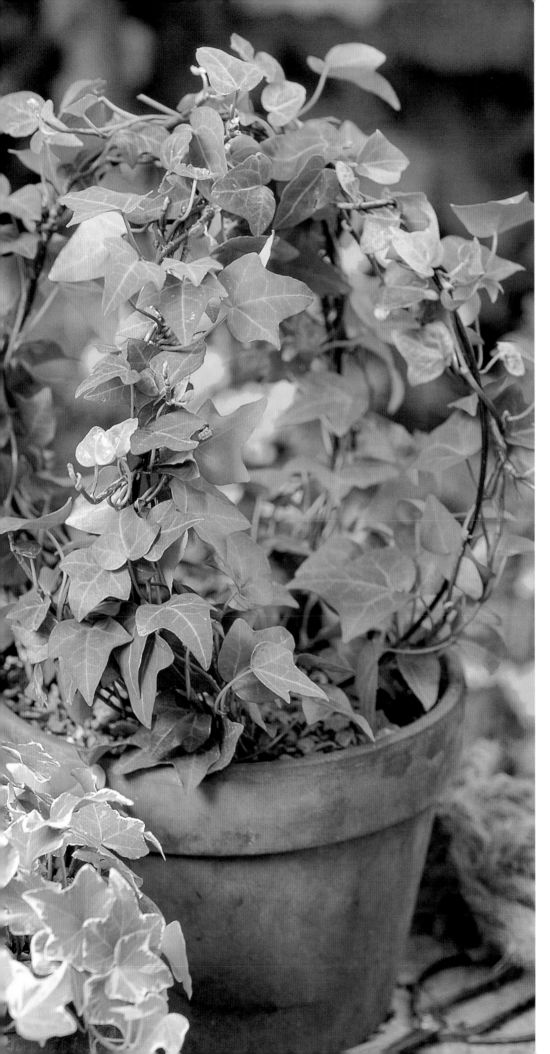

left: *The little globe in its first season. The shoots will gradually flesh out the shape more distinctly as the straggling shoots are tucked in or snipped off.*

right: *A small ivy pyramid makes the ideal choice of topiary for a shady corner, as few other plants will grow as well in this situation. This little pyramid is in its first year of growth.*

opposite: *A small pyramid created from a mixture of ivy and clematis. Even in its early stages, the pyramid still has architectural merit.*

FALSE TOPIARY PYRAMID

JUST LIKE THE BOX pyramid shown on page 30, ivy pyramids lend a classical feel to any garden. Since they are relatively quick growing, they are a good means of achieving height in a planting scheme, particularly as the container in which they are set is above ground level. For larger pyramids, you can choose ivies with larger leaves, such as 'Glacier'. For quick results, use those that grow fast (see page 89). Because almost all ivies, except those with variegated leaves, will cope well with very low light levels, a pyramid composed of them is the ideal choice for a shady balcony, porch or backyard.

The pyramid shape is an easy one to construct yourself (see below). For good coverage it pays to make one out of chicken wire and fill the shape with moss.

How to make an ivy pyramid

For the topiary pyramid shown left you will need three good-sized small-leaved ivy plants (about 20cm/8in tall) and a suitably sized container (around 30cm/12in in diameter and depth). You will also need a pyramid-shaped frame, some reel wire and a pair of scissors.

1 Plant up the container with the ivy plants evenly spaced around the perimeter. Insert the pyramid-shaped guide over the container.

2 Using reel wire, criss cross the struts of the frame to provide additional support for the ivy shoots as they grow. Keep the plants well watered and fed to encourage growth.

3 As the plants grow, train them by twisting them around the struts of the frame. Once the frame is well covered, the ivy can be clipped to create a dense, neat shape.

FALSE TOPIARY SPIRAL

AS MOST CLIMBING plants are vigorous, they will quickly cover a tall frame, such as a spiral, in one or two seasons. Ivy is the most popular choice, as it not only grows fast but bushes out well, rapidly disguising the metal frame. There is no complicated pruning or shaping with false topiary forms: all you have to do is to train the new shoots around the curves of the frame, tying in the more wayward ones using plastic plant ties, and tucking any stray smaller ones into the general growth. Among the more rapidly growing ivies for this kind of topiary are cultivars of *Hedera helix*, such as 'Congesta', 'Erecta' and 'Pedata'.

If you wish to make your own spiral frame, you can do so by winding a couple of lengths of heavy-duty wire around an appropriately sized cone. Then remove the cylinder and bind the lengths of wire together at intervals. Attach a couple of stout wires to the base to form an anchoring point.

opposite: *This 1.2m- (4ft-) tall topiary spiral was created using three ivy plants, the leading shoots of which were then trained up the spiral frame. Once the shoots fill the frame, they can be trimmed with garden shears a couple of times a year to keep the outline neat and dense.*

How to make an ivy spiral

You will need a spiral frame and a suitable pot (for example, for a 1.2m-/4ft-spiral you will need a 23cm-/8in-diameter pot) and two to three ivy plants. Insert the frame in the chosen pot, making sure it is well-anchored in the compost. Plant up in the usual way (see page 22), inserting the plants at the base of the first coil.

1 Once the ivy has started to grow upwards, train the new shoots by tucking them under the existing ones or tying them in.

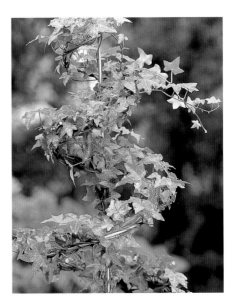

2 When the ivy reaches the top of the spiral and the wire frame is fully covered, clip the structure neatly a couple of times during the growing season.

right: Viola 'Jackanapes' is a small-flowered purplish-blue and yellow pansy that is ideal for this kind of topiary treatment. Larger flowered pansies do not keep their shape as well, and the flowers are too blousy.

FLOWER PYRAMID

opposite: This is a completed topiary pansy pyramid in which three tiered pots are placed on top of each other. In a very short space of time, the plants will grow together and disguise the underlying pyramid structure.

AS WELL AS the more traditional false topiary made from fast-growing creepers such as ivy you can make topiary-like pyramids from small flowering plants with a fairly lax growth habit. They can be planted up to echo the formal topiary pyramid shape, using a tiered arrangement of three pots, with the largest at the base and the smallest at the top. They make an attractive and sympathetic addition to an evergreen topiary display, although they are not a permanent feature, and will last only as long as the normal flowering season of the plant. Once the flowering season is over, dismantle the structure and feed and water the plants well until required the following year.

Among the best plants for this kind of treatment are small-flowered pansies (*Viola* sp.), *Bacopa* sp. (which produces a looser effect) and little grape hyacinths (*Muscari* sp.). The secret to keeping the display looking good is to ensure it does not suffer from excessive heat or drought. Keep it in partial shade and water it well at all times. Feed once a fortnight to prolong flowering, and deadhead for the same purpose.

How to create a flower pyramid

You will need to assemble three pots, ideally with a difference in diameter of about 5cm (2in) each. The largest should be about 23cm (8in) across and the smallest 10cm (4in) in diameter. Eighteen or so young pansy plants should be about right for this size of structure. You will also need enough potting medium to fill the three pots, and a small trowel.

opposite: *A less formal version using the same principle but with* Bacopa *'Snowflake' as a substitute for the pansies.*

1 Start to build the underlying structure. Half fill the largest container with compost and position the next size of container in the middle of it. Partially fill the sides with compost.

2 Start to add the individual plants around the base of the second pot (about five or six will be sufficient for this size of container).

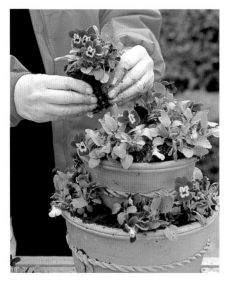

3 You can then add the plants to the second container, around its edges, after partially filling it with compost.

4 Finally site the last pot in the centre of the middle pot and plant it up with one or two plants, as needed. Water very thoroughly and keep well watered and fed.

TOPIARY CHAIR

opposite: *This ladder back chair has had panels of foliage plants inserted into the seat and up the back. Occasional clipping will help to create a neat, more sculpted appearance.*

ECCENTRIC FIGURES and fanciful items, from a chess set to a fox hunt, complete with fox, hounds and horses, have long been the preserve of topiary specialists and can be seen in many of the great gardens. For those who want a slightly whimsical element to their topiary, but do not want to spend too long in the process, a simple topiary chair seat can be fun to create. The idea could be adapted easily for a bench as well.

The one shown here is created from chamomile (*Anthemis nobilis* 'Treneague') which is a tough small plant that makes a dense mat of foliage fairly quickly. It can be sat upon without doing it any permanent damage. As it is a herb, it is also pleasantly aromatic and has medicinal properties, so if you feel so inclined, you could make a tisane out of the clippings!

How to make a topiary seat

You will need an old chair with a slot-in seat. For the seat you will need a piece of board or metal with holes punctured in it, cut to fit the seat slot in the chair, some chicken wire cut to dimensions roughly 10cm (4in) larger all round that the seat, a plastic liner and a bucket of compost. To fill a board 45cm (18in) square you will need approximately nine plants.

1 Put the board in the centre of the chicken wire and turn up the edges of the wire to make a narrow surround. Cover this with black plastic with a few holes punctured in it.

2 Fill this with compost and plant up the plants at evenly spaced intervals. Water the plants in well.

3 Transfer the board to the seat and fit it into the slot. Allow the plants to grow until they cover the compost, and then trim twice a season in spring and summer.

DISPLAYING
topiary

Topiary can be used to enhance many very different situations, from balconies and roof terraces to paths and flights of steps, for example. Although the primary goal with topiary is to create an elegant classical display, its neat symmetry will help to give unity and cohesion to more loosely organized groups of flowering containers, as well. You can use quick-growing evergreen climbers for false topiary to produce more rapid results.

THE WAYS IN WHICH you can use topiary vary greatly, but since its primary feature is its classic simplicity, it pays to introduce an element of formality into the design. Symmetrical designs are the most popular and are ideally suited to any formal setting. Pairs of container topiary pots are often used to flank a doorway, or to mark the beginning of a path. Series of pots can be lined up either side of a path, or along a windowsill or on top of a wall.

Since its form is its main attribute, you need to pay attention to the scale of the setting, ensuring that the topiary shapes enhance any architecture that frames them. Larger topiaries can be used to emphasize perspective, or to draw attention to a vista or a view.

In less formal settings, topiary can be used as a focal point, to bring a sense of cohesion and unity to an unruly mass of flowers either with a single tall topiary feature or by containing more inhibited planting within a neat surround of geometric shapes.

More fanciful topiary shapes – exotic beasts and birds – can add humour and vitality to a more sober display, and they can act as a conversation piece on a patio or terrace.

The restrained and elegant lines of the topiary usually demand a similarly elegant container, but rules are made to be broken and if you want to play visual games, you can combine classic topiary shapes with surprising containers, galvanized steel window boxes or recycled packing cases (see page 28) to produce a minimal, modern look.

right: This front garden has made good use of different topiaries in containers to lend structure and dignity to the planting. A pair of box balls flank the front door, while tall clipped yews stand sentinel at the entrance to the path. Clipped hedging flanks the path, the curve of the stone ball contrasting with its neatly rectangular lines, and echoing the shape of the box balls by the door.

right: *In this long
narrow garden, two topiary
box domes mark the
transition between one
compartment of the garden
and the next, their form
echoed in a larger pair of
clipped privets. Putting the
larger forms behind the
smaller ones gives a sense
of false perspective,
effectively foreshortening
the garden.*

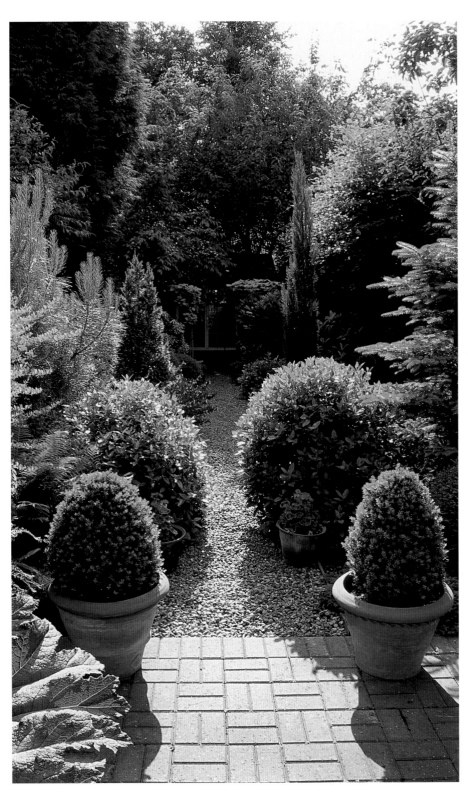

FRAMING A VIEW

TOPIARY HAS LONG BEEN used in classical garden design to emphasize perspective and to make the most of long vistas. You can bring a touch of elegance to any garden by introducing neatly symmetrical pairs or groups of container topiary. Raising the topiary shapes on a plinth will help to add height, saving many years' growing time.

Useful design concepts include introducing contrasts of shape and form and positioning fancy spirals and pompoms against the vertical lines of pergolas, columns or doorways. Use smaller balls or pyramids in yew or box to lead the eye down a path towards a central focal point at its end.

below: In this classically inspired Irish garden, two matching pairs of handsome box spirals flank a small classical temple, drawing attention to its elegant lines.

DOORWAYS

above: *A small summer house in Gothic style has been given a more imposing entrance with the addition of two generously sized topiary balls. They link the more formal style of the garden with the rustic charm of the little summer house, its roof awash with wisteria in early summer.*

opposite: *This attractive colonial house has made clever use of both climbers and neatly clipped topiaries. The combination of formality and informality echoes the style of the architecture, a blend of classical with romantic.*

THE ARCHITECTURAL FEATURES of your house provide an excellent setting for topiary, and none better than doorways which provide the ideal backdrop to a display of neatly clipped geometric shapes. The nature and style of the display will be dictated by the style of the architecture, and the surrounding space.

If you have an elegant period town house, for example, then a pair of matching pyramids in handsome containers are the perfect choice for the doorstep. A country house, with an expanse of terrace next to the door, allows you more scope and you can create a mixed display of pompoms, spirals, cones and pyramids (see page 39).

It is important to make sure the scale looks appropriate, and, generally speaking, a handsome and imposing doorway is best set off with topiaries in a scale that does justice to it. Ideally, the height of the tallest topiary should be about one third the height of the doorway (remember that the pot will make up roughly one-third of that height itself).

To create year-round appeal, you can put a pair of matching standards either side of a doorway, and underplant them with small flowering perennials or annuals, ringing the changes season by season, or use evergreen foliage plants for a more permanent display. Helxine, thyme or chamomile can all be used to cover the surface of the container. If you decide not to plant up the container, then it is best to mulch the surface with some attractive material, such as mussel shells or coloured gravel.

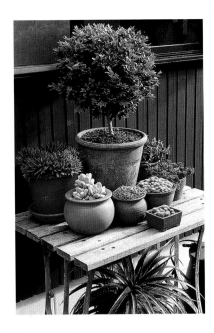

above: *A little topiary standard provides the centrepiece for a table top display, flanked by small architectural foliage plants in pots. Theming a display – in this case using foliage – helps to give it a sense of unity and cohesion.*

opposite: *Topiaries are ideal for balconies as they look good all year round and take up relatively little space. Combine them with luxuriant flowering climbers to achieve visual excitement with architectural elegance.*

BALCONIES

THE SLENDER SHAPES of topiary standards and pyramids are ideal for small spaces. Not only do they lend an air of sophistication to the planting, they also help to emphasize the lines of the architecture. Since they are relatively low maintenance, and both box and bay are fairly drought resistant, they are a handsome planting choice, but exceptionally easy to look after.

If you create staging, such as a couple of wirework shelves, you will be able to give the planting additional interest by staggering the heights of the containers. Neat rows of box balls in matching pots on a simple shelf, with a flowering standard, such as a fuchsia or rose, positioned at each end, take up very little space while creating a display that is not only smart but durable. You can underplant the standards with short-lived displays of bulbs and annuals, ideally colour-themed to give a sense of unity to the scheme – one such planting plan might be an all-white one of 'Triumphator' tulips in spring, followed by white busy lizzies in summer, white cyclamens in autumn and white heathers in the winter months.

When underplanting topiary you need to be careful to echo its simplicity of form so that the whole design looks harmonious. A stately topiary underplanted with blousy flowers looks rather like a dowager dressed in a unsuitably frilly skirt! As the essence of topiary is understated elegance, this concept needs to apply to any subsidiary planting too.

Ivies can be used to give a sense of movement to the planting if the topiary looks too static, but the smaller, dark-leaved ivies tend to combine better with it than the larger, floppier-leaved ones.

If you are planning to use quite large topiaries, or a fair number of them, it is important to consult a structural engineer to make sure that the balcony can carry the load successfully. Very high balconies may need some screening system to counter the effect of cold winds. You must also make sure there is an adequate drainage system to carry away surplus water.

WINDOWSILLS

above: *A small window ledge houses a little terracotta window box with a central tiny topiary ball, in the process of growing to its eventual size, with variegated ivies and pansies.*

opposite: *For a modern setting, a straightsided metal window box has been given an architectural treatment with ornamental cabbages, planted either side of a large box ball.*

IF YOU WANT a smart, easy to maintain planting scheme for windowsills, you need look no further than topiary! You can choose from traditional topiary forms and plants or more modern ones, but the windowsill makes an ideal stage on which to display a collection of topiary. You can play with the combinations of shapes to achieve all kinds of interesting effects, whether all foliage displays or combinations of foliage and flowers. The former can offer a sense of harmony and unity with different topiary shapes created from one type of plant (box is the most commonly used) or you can play with texture by using the same shape for each topiary, but using different plants. Some sense of symmetry is extremely important, however, as the geometric forms of topiary are lost without it.

One of the best schemes is to use a small topiary shape as the central plant in a window box, and then change the flanking plants each season. This way the window box has structure but you enjoy the benefits of a changing display. For a very low maintenance scheme, you can simply create rows of identical topiary shapes in attractive pots, be they plain terracotta, metal or subtly painted. Witty ideas include a series of playing card topiaries – a heart, diamond, spade and club shape created from wire around which ivy is then trained.

Another successful solution is to alternate small pots of clipped box with similar pots of a single flower, such as the handsome dark-leaved, pink-flowered *Primula* 'Guinevere' or an elegant pansy like the nearly black *Viola* 'Mollie Sanderson'.

If you are growing your own plants from cuttings, you can pot each up in its own small terracotta pot, lining up rows of these cuttings on the window ledge, perhaps painting the pots in alternating colours – white and black would produce a classical look. In this way, you succeed in using the available space to great effect.

If you are using several containers on a windowledge, make sure that they are of the same material or colour, or are combined in some other considered manner. In a limited space it is imperative that every inch counts.

On upper storey windowsills, to prevent pots from being blown off the ledge (and possibly causing damage to other people or their property), install some kind of restraining lip or, if you can afford it, an attractive railing.

DIRECTORY
of plants

Those plants commonly used in topiary, both for clipped forms and for training as climbers, are included on the following pages. The individual entries for each plant are in Latin name order. Each one includes the following information: common name (where applicable), hardiness, height in containers, suitable cultivars or varieties, position, cultivation, propagation and any pests and diseases to which they may be subject.

ARGYRANTHEMUM FRUSTESCENS
Marguerite
Half-hardy
Height 1.2m (4ft)
Bushy woody-stemmed perennials, marguerites have single white typical daisy flowers with a golden central disc. The foliage is silvery green and finely divided. Cultivars come in different colours, including the bright pink 'Vancouver' and the yellow 'Jamaica Primrose' and 'Cornish Gold'. These plants make good standards. You will need to pinch out the shoot tips to encourage the head to bush out once the plant reaches the appropriate height. Marguerites prefer sun. You can propagate them from semi-ripe cuttings taken in early autumn. Feed monthly with a seaweed-based fertilizer during the growing season. They are generally pest and disease free.

BUXUS
Box
Hardy
Height 1.2m (4ft)
There are several species of box, the best known being *B. sempervirens* (common box). It has small, oval, evergreen leaves. There are cultivars with variegated leaves, and the leaves also vary in size according to the species and cultivar. The smallest leaved box is *B. microphylla*. Most grow to around 1.2m (4ft) but there are also dwarf and low-growing forms. Of the many cultivars of *B. sempervirens*, 'Handsworthiensis' is one of the best known. Being vigorous, it is a good choice for topiary as it will create the shapes you require more quickly than some other forms. It will put on up to 10-15cm (4-6in) of growth a year. 'Suffruticosa', which has small neat leaves, is also widely used for topiary.
Box prefers sun or light shade and will cope with fairly minimal watering. You can propagate box easily from heeled cuttings taken in summer or early autumn. Clip twice a year in early and midsummer for a neat

finish. Although box is easy to grow, it has recently become prone to attacks from a fungal disorder, for which there is no cure. It is less likely to succumb if grown with plenty of air circulating around the plant, and container-grown specimens seem to be damaged less than box hedges, particularly those that are grown under trees.

CEANOTHUS
California lilac
Half-hardy to hardy
Height 3m (10ft)
There is a wide range of species and cultivars, some evergreen, some deciduous, and some hardier than others. Choose the hardy ever-greens for standards. *Ceanothus* 'Autumnal Blue' is a good choice, with its small, dark evergreen leaves and its mid-blue small panicles of flowers from early to late summer. Of the deciduous ceanothus, you could try 'Gloire de Versailles' with its attractive dark blue flowers. Use either to make standards up to a height of 1.5m (5ft). The evergreen ceanothus will need only light pruning once the standard shape has been achieved. Deciduous plants should have the lateral shoots pruned back to a couple of outward facing buds after flowering. Propagate from semi-ripe cuttings in summer. Ceanothus is fairly pest and disease resistant.

COPROSMA X KIRKII
'VARIEGATA'
Tender
Height 1.2m (4ft)
This tender, spreading, low-growing shrub would seem an unlikely candidate for training into a standard, but successful small standards can be created from it, with a pret-tily arching head, similar to the willow (*Salix x caprea*) shown on page 57. The leaves are small and almost needlelike, a palish green edged with silver. If you grow a pair of male and female plants, mistletoe-like berries are

borne in autumn. It will need to be overwintered indoors in winter in colder climates. The leading shoot of the standard will need to be staked to encourage it to grow straight. Feed the plant with a seaweed-based fertilizer at monthly intervals. Pinch out the shoot tips to encourage a more bushy head to the standard. Propagate from semi-ripe cuttings in late summer. They are generally pest and disease free.

x CUPRESSOCYPARIS LEYLANDII
Leyland cypress
Hardy
Height 9m (10ft) in containers
This is very tough conifer which is quick growing, but makes a good candidate for upright topiaries, such as pyramids and spirals. The leaves are needle-like and glossy green. The compact, slower-growing *C.l.* 'Fletcheri' has greyish-green feathery foliage. It should be planted in ericaceous compost as conifers prefer acid soil. It will need trimming two or three times anually, in spring and in early and late summer. It can be propagated from semi-ripe cuttings taken either in spring or in summer and it is generally pest and disease free.

CUPRESSUS
Cypress
Hardy
Height 3-4m (10-13ft)
These slender, upright, fast-growing conifers with their dense foliage make excellent topiary specimens and can also be trained as standards. There are forms with golden foliage, including *C. macrocarpa* 'Goldcrest'. Trains easily into pyramids, and can also be trained, less easily, into spirals. Plant them up using an ericaceous compost, as conifers prefer acid soil. Propagate in either early autumn or in spring from softwood cuttings. Cypresses are generally found to be pest and disease free.

Buxus sempervirens

Hedera helix 'Glacier'

Ilex aquifolium

FUCHSIA
Half-hardy to hardy
Height 1.5m (5ft)
These bushy deciduous shrubs, with small oval mid-green leaves, are extremely floriferous with double or single flowers consisting of outer sepals with tubular dangling petals inside, often in a different colour. Colourways include carmine and purple, pink and white, deep cerise and pale pink. Different hybrids and species have varying degrees of hardiness. They make excellent standards but the stem will need to be staked. Of the many hybrids you can choose, 'Granma Sinton' has pale pink semi-double petals and lighter pink sepals. 'Winston Churchill' has deep purple petals with rich pink sepals. They do well in sun or part shade. Propagate from semi-ripe cuttings in summer. Prone to aphid attacks; spray with derris at first signs of attack.

HEDERA HELIX
Common ivy
Hardy
Height 3m (10ft) or more
There are many different species and cultivars of ivy, a vigorous evergreen climber, but those that are most suitable for container growing for quick topiary are the more vigorous ones such as 'Erecta', 'Oro di Bogliasco', *H.h. pedata* and *H.h. f. poetarum*. Less vigorous varieties are 'Conglomerata' and 'Goldchild'. Those with small, neat leaves make good choices for more complex shapes, but the gold- and silver-variegated varieties, such as 'Goldheart' and 'Glacier', make an attractive alternative although their variegation may revert to plain-coloured leaves in shade. Otherwise ivies do well in shady conditions. Ivy roots very easily, whenever it touches soil, so propagation is very easy: you can often simply detach an already rooted stem or take cuttings in late summer. Ivy can sometimes be prone to red spider mite, but frequent misting with water helps prevent attacks.

ILEX
Holly
Half-hardy to hardy
Height 3m (10ft)
There is a vast range of species and cultivars in this group of trees and shrubs, which make excellent standards as the foliage is evergreen and very dense. Although we are familiar with the dark, glossy green spiny leaves of holly, there are many variegated forms, and some that have no spines to the leaves. Depending on their place of origin, hollies vary in hardiness. One of the most commonly grown is *I. aquifolium* (the common holly or English holly) which has many variegated cultivars. 'Argentea Marginata' has silver variegated spiny leaves. 'Golden Queen' has broad leaves with a dark green centre and yellow margins. If you grow a pair of male and female plants, you will get bright red berries in autumn. Hollies do best in sun. Propagate from semi-ripe cuttings taken in summer. Hollies are fairly pest resistant but can be prone to powdery mildews.

LAURUS NOBILIS
Bay
Half-hardy
Height 3m (10ft)
This evergreen tree is deservedly popular for topiary and for standards. The oval, glossy very dark green leaves are aromatic (and often used in cooking to flavour soups and stews). As a tree, it makes a strong, firm stem for a standard (which can be trained up to

Laurus nobilis

Lavandula officinalis

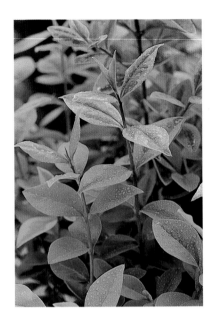

Ligustrum ovalifolium

2m/6ft tall), generally putting on about 23cm (9in) of growth a year, so it is fairly quick growing. It has small, inconspicuous yellow flowers in late spring, followed by small black fruits. In cold areas, you may need to provide winter protection by bubble-wrapping the container. It prefers a sunny position. Propagate from semi-ripe cuttings in summer. Bay can be prone to attacks from scale insect. Spray with malathion at the first sight of an attack (evidenced by the leaves starting to curl, with a white powdery substance inside the curled leaf) because it can quickly spread to the whole bush.

LAVANDULA ANGUSTIFOLIA
Lavender
Half-hardy
Height 90cm (3ft)
This well-known herb with its evergreen, silver-green needle like leaves makes an attractive small flowering standard, although the head tends to be less spherical and the leading shoot will need staking to produce a strong stem. Depending on the hybrid or variety, small light to dark purple fragrant spires of flowers are produced from early to late summer. Lavender is a great attraction for bees. It prefers a sunny position. Propagate from semi-ripe cuttings in summer. Lavender is generally pest and disease free.

LIGUSTRUM OVALIFOLIUM
Privet
Hardy
Height 2m (6ft)
This tough evergreen is used widely for topiary. It is often used in place of box, being much quicker growing, but will need more regular clipping. There are gold and white variegated cultivar, such as 'Aureum' and 'Argenteum'. Plant in sun or partial shade. White, pungent smelling flowers appear in summer. You can propagate it from semi-ripe cuttings in summer, or hardwood cuttings in winter. Generally trouble free.

LONICERA NITIDA
Boxleaf honeysuckle
Half hardy
Height 2m (6ft)
Similar in appearance to box, with small, dark evergreen leaves, it is quicker growing. The golden-leaved cultivar 'Baggesen's Gold' is less vigorous than the species and the leaves may scorch in strong sunlight. It will make good topiary specimens, ideal for pyramids, and is often used for standards, too. Insignificant white flowers are borne in summer, followed by purple berries in autumn. It will put on 15-23m (6-9in) of growth a year, so will need clipping two to three times from summer to autumn to keep topiaries in shape. It prefers sun (except for golden forms) or partial shade. Propagate from semi-ripe cuttings in late summer. Generally trouble free.

MYRTUS COMMUNIS
Myrtle
Tender
Height 2m (6ft)
This aromatic evergreen shrub is used for both topiaries and standards, the neat small leaves being a dark glossy green and dense. It offers the bonus of scented white flowers from early to late summer. Being tender, it will need protection in winter in colder climates. It prefers a sunny position. Feed with a seaweed-based fertilizer during the growing season. Clip after flowering. You can

Prunus sp.

Rosmarinus officinalis

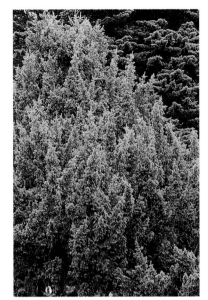

Taxus baccata 'Elegantissima'

propagate it from semi-ripe cuttings taken in the summer.

PELARGONIUM
Geranium
Tender
Height 1.8m (6ft) or more
There are various groups of pelargonium but generally the zonal ones will make good standards. Tender perennials, but treated like annuals in cold climates, they have attractive, lobed leaves with markings in various colours from wine-purple to white. The leaves release a pungent scent when crushed. The flowers are produced over a long period from early summer right through to the first frosts, and come in many different shades, from almost black through various reds and pinks to white. To train pelargoniums as standards, you will need a conservatory or greenhouse as they will have to be overwintered. Propagate from shoot tips in summer, and then grow the cuttings under cover in winter, removing the sideshoots, but not all the side leaves, until the plant reaches the required height, when the leading shoot should be pinched out, and the sideshoots below it con-

tinually pinched until the mop-head forms. Pelargoniums are generally trouble free, but the leaves will yellow if they are overwatered.

PRUNUS LAUROCERASUS
Laurel
Hardy
Height 3m (10ft)
A dense evergreen shrub, laurel has long narrow dark green leaves with fragrant white flowers in mid-spring, followed by small red fruit (hence its other common name, cherry laurel). There are a number of varieties, including a variegated one, 'Marbled White' (formerly called 'Castlewellan'). It can be used to create mophead standards or small topiary pyramids. It will do well in both full sun and partial shade. Prune it in spring. Prone to aphid attacks.

ROSA
Rose
Hardy
Height 1.5m (5ft)
This is a huge genus with its marvellous array of species and hybrid shrubs and climbers with flowers that range from single todouble;

some are very densely packed, known as quartered. Almost all are richly fragrant. 'Ballerina', a hybrid musk rose, makes a neat standard with double pink flowers. While normal standards are up to 1.5m (5ft) tall, you can also grow patio roses as much smaller standards, only 60cm (2ft) tall. You can also create weeping standards from climbers and ramblers, often trained over an umbrella-shaped wire frame. The technique for creating the standards is as for the fuchsia on page 53. Pruning will vary depending on the type of rose used for the mop-head but as a general rule cut out any diseased or crossing stems in late winter and then cut back vigorous shoots to 15m (6in) and lateral shoots to 4-6in (10-15cm) in spring. Prone to blackspot and to aphids.

ROSMARINUS OFFICINALIS
Rosemary
Half-hardy
Height 1.5m (5ft)
This aromatic evergreen shrub is also a much loved herb. The small needlelike leaves are glaucous grey-green, emitting a pungent aroma when crushed, and the flowers, from

Thuja plicata 'Variegata'

Viburnum plicatum

Viola x *wittrockiana*

spring to early summer, are small, tubular and pale blue-mauve. Rosemary can be used to create small flowering standards. You can propagate it easily from heel cuttings in summer. It prefers a sunny spot, and will cope well with drought. Generally trouble free.

Salix
Willow
Hardy
Height variable
There are many different species and varieties of willow, characterized in spring by attractive catkins and slender, often arching or drooping branches. For the purposes of topiary, train the creeping willows, such as *S. repens* (see page 57) to make small, attractively branched small standards. Willows prefer to be kept moist in a sunny position. Can be attacked by aphids, caterpillars, leaf beetles and sawflies.

Taxus baccata
Yew
Hardy
Height 3m (10ft)
The common yew is a popular evergreen for topiary. It is slow growing and its very dark needlelike leaves create a dense, uniform structure. The flowers are inconspicuous but small red (and poisonous) berries appear in autumn and winter. Yew puts on about 23cm (8in) of growth a year. It is well suited to topiary pyramids, which suits its natural growth habit. It will grow in both sunny and shady situations. Trim it back by 10cm (4in) or so in summer and early autumn. Generally found to be trouble free.

Thuja
Hardy
Height 4m (13ft) or more
This tough conifer is an evergreen, with very dark scale-like leaves. It makes a good subject for topiary. Cultivars of species such as *T. orientalis* have the dense foliage necessary. Some cultivars have golden foliage, such as 'Elegantissima'. *Thuja occidentalis* has foliage that is apple-scented. *Thuja occidentalis* 'Holmstrup' has mid-green leaves. Plant in ericaceous compost in sun or partial shade. Trim back by 10cm (4in) or more in spring and late summer. Can be prone to scale insects and also to attacks by aphids.

Viburnum
Hardy
Height 2m (6ft)
The evergreen species and cultivars make good standards. They have small, oval, dark green leaves and flattish heads of tiny white or pinkish flowers in late winter or early spring. Some species have scented flowers. The flowers are often followed by small black fruits. *Viburnum plicatum* and *V. tinus lauristinus* make good standards. Plant them in sun or partial shade. Propagate by semi-ripe cuttings in summer. Watch out for aphids and whiteflies.

Viola x wittrockiana
Pansy
Hardy
Height 15cm (6in)
Pansies make good subjects for instant floral topiaries, as the flowers will last over a long season; there are both winter-, spring- and summer-flowering pansies. They cope with partial shade but prefer sun. They need frequent watering and feeding. Grow from seed sown in early spring. Can be prone to attacks by aphids and to mildews.

GLOSSARY

Annual *Plant that completes its life cycle in one season.*

Biennial *Plant that completes its life cycle in two years, growing in the first year, and flowering and fruiting in the second.*

Cambium *Layer of cells between the bark and the wood which actively produces cells, and from which new cells will grow in the process known as grafting.*

Deciduous *Plant that sheds its leaves annually, at the onset of lower light levels and cooler temperatures.*

Central leader *The vertical and dominant stem at the centre of a tree.*

Crown *The upper branches and foliage of a tree.*

Cultivar *A cultivated variety of plant produced by horticultural plant breeding techniques.*

Deadheading *The removal of spent flowers, to encourage more new buds to form.*

Dormant *The stage in the annual cycle of growth, usually in autumn and winter, when the plant activity slows down or stops.*

Espalier *A form of training in which the lateral branches of a tree are trained horizontally.*

Evergreen *Said of a plant that is not deciduous, i.e. does not lose its leaves in winter.*

Family *A botanical term for a group of plants sharing similar characteristics.*

Fan *A form of training in which the lateral branches of a tree are trained at a 45° angle to the main stem.*

Genus *A subdivision of a family of plants, made up of species, hybrids and cultivars that share closely related characteristics.*

Grafting *Process by which a shoot or single bud on one plant (technically termed the scion) can be united with the root system and stem of another plant (known as the rootstock or stock) to produce a plant that combines the characteristics of both plants.*

Half-hardy *Term used to describe a plant that is not reliably hardy, but may withstand temperatures just below freezing for short periods.*

Hardy *Term used to describe a plant that can withstand temperatures below freezing for periods of time.*

Hybrid *A cross between two or more species, denoted with a 'x' in botanical names.*

Lateral *A subsidiary shoot growing from a larger stem.*

Leader
See Central leader

Pinching out *To remove the tip of a shoot; it prevents further growth of that stem, and encourages laterals lower down to grow, creating a more bushy plant.*

Rootstock *The term used to describe the lower plant in grafting, which forms the roots of the combined plants.*

Scion *The term used to describe the upper plant in grafting, which is combined with the rootstock of another plant.*

Sideshoot *A small shoot growing from a lateral or a main stem.*

Species *A subdivision of a genus, which can be further subdivided into subspecies, cultivars and varieties.*

Standard *A tree or shrub trained to produce several feet of clear stem above which the upper branches are pruned into a ball shape.*

Tender *Term used to describe a plant that cannot withstand temperatures below freezing.*

Tipping *See Pinching out*

Variety *A naturally occurring variant of a species.*

SUPPLIERS

UK

Avant Garden
77 Ledbury Road
London W11 2AG
Tel: 020 7229 4408
www.avantgardenshop.com

Burgon and Ball Ltd
La Plata Works, Holme Lane
Sheffield S6 4JY
Tel: 01442 338262
www.burgonandball.com

Capital Garden Products
Gibbs Reed Bar, Ticehurst
East Sussex TN5 7HE
Tel: 01580 201092
www.capital-garden.com

Ferndale Lodge
Woodview Road, Paignton
Devon TQ4 7NG
Tel: 01803 696 500
www.ferndale-lodge.co.uk

Fibrex Nurseries Ltd
Honeybourne Road
Tabworth, Stratford upon Avon
Warwickshire CV37 8XT
Tel: 01789 720788
www.fibrex.co.uk

Langley Boxwood Nursery
Rake, Nr Liss,
Hampshire GU33 7JL
Tel: 01730 894467
www.boxwood.co.uk

The Romantic Garden
The Street, Swannington, Norwich
Norfolk NR9 5NW
Tel: 01603 261488
www.romantic-garden-nursery.co.uk

Traditional Garden Supply Company
Cotswold House, 1 Crompton Road
Groundwell Industrial Estate
Swindon, Wiltshire SN25 5AR
Tel: 0870 600 3366
www.scottsofstow.co.uk

Wadham Trading Company
Digbeth Street, Stow on the Wold
Gloucestershire GL54 1BN
Tel: 01451 830308
www.wadhamtrading.co.uk

AUSTRALIA

Earthworks Nursery
1490 Grasstree Hill Road
Richmond, TAS 7025
Tel: (03) 6260 2770

Essendon Garden Centre
1060 Mt Alexander Road
Essendon, VIC 3040
Tel: (03) 9379 0555

Flower Power Garden Centre
124 Newbridge Road
Moorebank, NSW 2170
Tel: (02) 9601 4555

Garden Elegance
150 Railway Road

Subiaco, WA 6008
Tel: (08) 9381 2197

NEW ZEALAND

King's Plant Barn, Auckland
Forrest Hill, tel: (09) 410 4139
Howick, tel: (09) 273 8527
Remuera, tel: (09) 524 9400
St Lukes, tel: (09) 846 2141
Silverdale, tel: (09) 426 0401
Takapunka, tel: (09) 443 2221
www.kings.co.nz

Palmers Gardenworld
Glenfield
Tel: (09) 443 9910
www.palmers.co.nz

McCully's Garden Centres
Tel: (03) 351 7128
www.garden.co.nz

BIBLIOGRAPHY

Garden Craftmanship in Yew and Box, *Nathaniel Lloyd* (Ernest Benn Ltd, London, 1925)

Quick and Easy Topiary and Green Sculpture, *Jenny Hendy* (Little, Brown and Company, London, 1996)

Topiary and the Art of Training Plants, *David Joyce* (Frances Lincoln, London, 1999)

The Complete Book of Topiary, *Barbara Gallup and Deborah Reich* (Workman, New York, 1987)

INDEX

ACKNOWLEDGEMENTS

Susan Berry would like to thank the following for their contribution to this book: **Steven Wooster** for his excellent photography, **Debbie Mole** for her elegant design, **Kate Simunek** for her sensitive artwork, and **LeeAnn Roots** for help with styling. The **Langley Boxwood Nursery**, in particular **Geraldine Veitch** and **Elizabeth Bainbridge**, for supplying plants and for checking information and the **Wadham Trading Company** for supplying frames. Thanks also to **Rosemary Wilkinson** and **Clare Johnson** of **New Holland**, and to **Marie Lorimer** for compiling the index.